Lifting the Veil

A FULL-LENGTH PLAY IN TWO ACTS

Lifting the Veil

A FULL-LENGTH PLAY IN TWO ACTS

TRINITY
HOUSE

PAUL D. PATTON

Integratio Press

Pasco, Washington

Trinity House is a Division of Integratio Press

www.integratiopress.com

Integratio Press is the Imprint of the Christianity and Communication Studies Network

11503 Easton Dr.
Pasco, WA 99301

www.theccsn.com

Cover design: Carol O'Callaghan
Cover composite image: Depositphotos graphics combined with manipulated photo of Richard Roberts and Kathryn Kuhlman ministering (OREA2000, CC BY-SA 4.0 www.creativecommons.org/licenses/by-sa/4.0> via Wikimedia Commons)
Interior design: Carol O'Callaghan

paperback isbn: 978-1-959685-27-2
ebook isbn: 978-1-959685-28-9

Library of Congress Control Number: 2025936269

Acknowledgments

THANKS TO MY FRIEND, Susan Reno, who commissioned me to write something for her to perform about Kathryn Kuhlman. We originally assumed it would be Susan dramatically reciting one of Kathryn's evangelistic and healing sermons. After reading the biographies, I realized there was a more demanding story.

About the Author

PAUL D. PATTON (PHD, REGENT UNIVERSITY) is Professor Emeritus of Communication and Theater at Spring Arbor University in Michigan. It was while pastoring at Trinity Church in Livonia, Michigan, that he founded Trinity House Theater in 1981. He is the author of over 30 produced stage plays, radio plays, and performance essays. He is contributing author to the books *Understanding Evangelical Media* (IVP), *Evangelical Christians and Popular Culture* (Praeger), and *Prophetic Critique and Popular Culture* (Peter Lang), and co-author of *Prophetically (In)Correct: A Christian Introduction to Media Criticism* (Brazos Press), and the newly published, *Everyday Sabbath: How to Lead Your Dance with Media and Technology in Mindful and Sacred Ways* (Cascade Books).

Synopsis

IN OCTOBER OF 1938, two evangelists/faith healers, Burroughs Walters and Kathryn Kuhlman, elope to Iowa to be married. The bride has fainted at the civil ceremony. The play covers the first one hundred minutes of their wedding night, the bride seriously second-guessing her decision to marry, feeling compelled to return to her flock in Denver. The bridegroom, frustrated on his wedding night, compels her to stay. *Lifting the Veil* is a play depicting the battle of two scripture-filled minds and wills.

Author's Notes

THE FOLLOWING PLAY is a "what-if" tale, loosely based upon the obscure marriage of Kathryn Kuhlman and Burroughs Waltrip. Burroughs became an early developer of Christian evangelistic radio ministry, while Kathryn, decades after her marriage, would hold evangelistic and faith-healing meetings that would draw crowds of tens of thousands. She became the most influential woman evangelist since Aimee Semple McPherson.

Here's what Kathryn Kuhlman's biographers tell us:

In 1938, Kathryn was in her early thirties and already the pastor of a thousand-member church she had founded in Denver. The itinerate evangelist and faith healer from Texas, Burroughs Waltrip, filled her pulpit twice—the first time for a month with his wife, Jessie, and two sons in tow, the second time sadly pronouncing that his wife had abandoned him and taken the boys, and a divorce was soon final. Kathryn and Burroughs subsequently fell in love, announced a merging of their ministries, and shortly afterward a union of their lives in wedlock. Kathryn fainted during her wedding vows. Upon awaking, the bridegroom helped her finish them. Kathryn would become possessed by forlornness over the internal tensions of a passionate love for Burroughs and the price-tag of her decision to marry—a decision that eventually closed the door on her ministry in Denver and required a submission to Burroughs's ministry vision in Iowa. The wedding night would provide the threshold to an intense collision course of biblical imagery, ministry vision, and the requirements of love.

For additional details, I recommend the following three biographies: Wayne Warner, *The Woman Behind the Miracles* (Ann Arbor, MI: Servant Publications, 1993); Jimmie McDonald, *The Kathryn Kuhlman I Knew* (Shippensburg, PA: Treasure House, 1996); and

Jamie Buckingham, *Daughter of Destiny* (North Brunswick, NJ: Bridge-Logos Press, 1999).

Historical Note

KATHRYN DID REFER to Burroughs as "Mister." As stiff and peculiar as this seems, it does give the play a more distinctive feel of another age.

I employ the last name "Walters" rather than "Waltrip" as a reminder that the play, though set up by events that did happen and a real collision course of two formidable souls, is not the result of a fly on the wall in that Iowa motel room who happened to have a microphone. Like other biographic extensions of speculation, this particular tale has employed informed guesses to fill in certain blanks.

Production Note

MY FRIEND, PAUL MURPHY, has written a beautifully haunting score for *Lifting the Veil*. In addition, the first and last movements—corresponding to the play's opening and closing silences—include recordings of Kathryn Kuhlman's radio sermons. Especially intriguing is the last movement, a slow, lilting rendition of the classic revivalist hymn, "The Solid Rock." Over the pensive melody, Ms. Kuhlman describes her key insight to finding the "will of God"—namely, "to have no will of your own." Copies of the score can be secured by contacting me at ppatton@arbor.edu.

Cast of Characters

IT'S OF VITAL IMPORTANCE to cast with utmost care for both main roles for a variety of reasons, not the least being they are on stage the whole length of the play. Additionally, both characters as faith-healing evangelists have roles in life that have been dismissively stereotyped—of course, not without some merit. But my desire is that both Kathryn and Burroughs would not become cartoonish confirmations of those convenient stereotypes.

Burroughs: In the original production at Spring Arbor University, I was privileged to cast a fine actor, Jared Cole, who possessed a young-John Goodman quality, i.e., very difficult to dislike. The dominant advantage was that the actor was able to engender empathy from the audience, without which the majority of the audience would only be identifying with Kathryn. It is essential the play remain a viable tension between two well-intended but flawed religious leaders. Crucial to this is avoiding the temptation to allow Burroughs to be too slick, or the other extreme—too much of a one-note, manipulative hick. It is also essential that the actor find the playfulness in any moment, especially the opportunities presented in each extemporaneous sermon. Burroughs can't help himself from this habit to default to a homily mode. His passion for all things might be best likened to Robert Duvall's *The Apostle* character in his film from the 1990s.

Kathryn: For the reader or audience member more familiar with Ms. Kuhlman's ministry, most would admit that Kathryn's could not be classified as a "hellfire and brimstone" style. Even during the pinnacle of her mass evangelistic work—as much as thirty years after the play setting—few would describe her as a passionate presence of memorable stridency or a golden-tongued master of preaching in any stereotypic way. The power of her hypnotic presence was not sourced in her commanding voice or demanding way, but more tied to a quieter willingness to lead, with hushed tones, her cherished throngs to the place of faithful anticipation at the movement of the Spirit. Hints of this should be evident in this play's depiction of a young Kathryn. More important to the effective portrayal is an actor's luminousness than commanding vocal presence. And it is important that the actor understand that Kathryn did deeply love Burroughs.

Cast List

Burroughs Walters (BW)	30s to mid-40ish Texan; passionate in a Robert Duval-*The Apostle* kind of way; itinerate evangelist and faith healer
Kathryn Kuhlman (KK)	Mid-20s to mid-30s, equally passionate, a native Kansan; pastored a large revivalist church in Denver; sensitive without being demure
Motel Manager (MM)	Any age, either male or female

Act One

SETTING: A motel bedroom, circa mid-30s-double bed, dresser,
lamp, mirror. Mid-October Iowa, 1938. A double bed
is placed upstage, center, with the foot of the bed fac-
ing downstage. Dresser with mirror is stage right of
the bed, a table and lamp is left of the bed. Two chairs
are farther stage left.

(BURROUGHS WALTERS, decked out in suit, enters
STAGE RIGHT, carrying a large bouquet of flowers in one
hand and suitcase in the other—places suitcase on dresser.
HE opens one of the suitcases, pulls out a woman's nightgown and lays it across the bed. Pulls out a woman's pair
of slippers and places them under the bed. Flowers still in
hand, HE looks for something to put them in.)

BW

(Calling offstage.)

Hold on, I'm tryin' to make it perfect. Wonderin' where I can put
this here bouquet? You'd think one soul spend five dollars on a
room they'd have an empty vase for flowers. Don't you think?

(HE waits for an answer. Nothing.)

BW (cont'd)

Darlin'? Don't ya' think?

(HE waits. Nothing. BW lays the flowers on the dresser,
tries to arrange them.)

BW (cont'd)

Look beautiful just lying there. One more thing, darlin'.

(BW opens HIS suitcase, removes cologne, applies it liberally to HIS face, looks in mirror.)

BW (cont'd)

You ready?

No answer.

BW (cont'd)

You gonna answer me sometime b'fore Christmas?

(BW exits.)

BW (cont'd)

(Offstage.)

Now you gone and done it again! I wanted you waitin' out here in the car so I could make it perfect in there! And now you gone and done it again! Now put y'arms round my neck. Darlin', sure would be a lot easier if you hadn't gone and

(Loud.)

DONE WHAT YOU DID!

(PAUSE.)

BW (cont'd)

(Toned down.)

Darlin', believe me I'm tryin' and I tried!

(BW enters, carrying in HIS arms KATHRYN, "across the threshold." HER coat covers HER wedding dress. A wedding veil remains over HER face.)

(HE lays HER across the foot of the bed. SHE lies there, motionless . . . unconscious. PAUSE. BW just looks at HER.)

BW (cont'd)

Ya' gonna take that coat off?

(No answer. BW sits on the bed.)

BW (cont'd)

Y'gonna take that veil off?

(Long PAUSE.)

BW (cont'd)

Don't suppose y'gonna take anything off.

(SHE lies motionless.)

BW (cont'd)

I'm talkin' to *you*, Misses Walters, Misses Kathryn Walters—sound good, don't it?

(HE moves closer.)

BW (cont'd)

Ol' boy, woulda skipped the little sermon if he'd really known who we were, don't ya' think, darlin'? Who ever heard of no justice of the peace preachin' no sermon? Don't ya' think? Couldn't follow it anyhow, 'specially after you fainted there in the middle. Yeh. Right there, ah, right there in the middle somehow. Scared me a little bit. Thought maybe you were sick . . . Are ya' sick? I sure ain't sick, no, sirree. And now ya' doin' it again. Two times faintin' in one night.

(HE steps toward the flowers, picks them up and brings them to HER.)

BW (cont'd)

Ya' like these flowers don't ya?

(Putting them under HER nose.)

BW (cont'd)

Smell mighty fine there, Misses Kathryn Walters.

(SHE remains motionless.)

BW (cont'd)

Fact is a lot of things smellin' mighty fine around here, young lady.

(Leaning toward HER.)

BW (cont'd)

You smell anything that fit your fancy? Do ya'? That's me you're smellin' I'll have you know. Yep. That's me you're smellin' on your weddin' night. New, brandy-spandy cologne I just splashed on. Yep.

> (No response. HE looks at HER, then off. PAUSE. HE starts to try to unbutton HER overcoat.)

BW (cont'd)

Darlin', now let me help ya' with this coat—now, c'mon there, bride—you're gonna have ta take somethin' off, and we might as well start with that there coat coverin' up that pretty weddin' dress.

> (SHE remains unconscious. HE puts HIS arm under HER back and tries to lift HER up into a sitting position, HIS other hand trying to unbutton the top buttons of HER coat.)
> (HE stops and tries to awaken HER by gently slapping the side of HER face.)

BW (cont'd)

C'mon, bride. Time to wake up Miss Kate.

> (It's not successful. HE unbuttons the coat until HE gets frustrated, HER unconscious arms not helping. He gets up from the bed; SHE slumps back on the mattress.)

BW (cont'd)

I know just the thing to do the trick.

> (HE exits.)

BW (cont'd)

> (Offstage.)

Yessiree, this'll do the trick.

> (HE enters carrying a glass of water. HE kneels beside HER, lifts HER veil.)

BW (cont'd)

Now darlin', I'm very sorry, and I don't ever wanna hurt ya', but I know of no other way to—

(HE pours the water from the glass, cascading on HER face. Then realizing . . . Really preaching.)

BW (cont'd)

Bap-tizin' you into holy, holy matrimony!

(SHE sits up, dazed, awakened, and not looking at HIM.)

BW (cont'd)

Well, say somethin' you who was buried in loneliness and raised with me in marital bliss! Say somethin'!

(SHE turns to HIM. PAUSE.)

KK

(Very groggy.)

What?

BW

What about what, Misses Kathryn Walters?

KK

We . . .

(Still coming out of it, looking down at wedding gown, realizing.)

I got married, didn't we?

BW

We sure did, sweetheart.

(SHE pulls veil back over HER face. BW moves toward HER, starts to draw veil away from HER face. SHE, more awake, grabs at the veil to pull it back over HER face, HE resists. SHE struggles.)

BW (cont'd)

Now darlin', no need—

(SHE bites HIS arm. BW shouts in pain. Pulls arm away.)

BW (cont'd)

Ooouuh! What in the name of—?

> (HE starts to roll up sleeve.)

BW (cont'd)

I bet you drew blood. My sweet Kate bites me on my wedding night, an hour after she faints at my weddin'.

> (HE sees there is no blood.)

BW (cont'd)

Sweet mama, I was 'bout to declare me part of the weddin' wounded, by golly, praise the Lord. I like a fight in a woman. Yep. Unpredictable, lively. I predict it'll make our love stronger, Kate my bride.

> (KK starts to cry, standing with veil over face.)

BW (cont'd)

Oh, darlin', I'm sorry, I know it's a hard thing to—

> (Interrupting HIMSELF.)

I'll bet you want your flowers, don't ya'?

> (BW runs to get the bouquet, brings them to HER. HE offers them to HER; SHE doesn't put out HER arms to take them. Arms remain at HER side; no offer to take them from BW.)

BW (cont'd)

You gonna take 'em, since they're yours?

> (HE tries to put them in HER arms. HE moves them in place.)

BW (cont'd)

Oooh, now ain't you a beautiful bride.

> (HE steps away, to get a full look at HIS new bride. SHE drops HER arms to the side; the bouquet falls to the floor.)

KK

My mama told me . . .

> (BW waits.)

BW

Now, now what yr'mama tell you, sweet thing. Spit it out, it's gonna be okay, halleluiah.

KK

W-when I was a little girl . . .

> (BW waits, KK muttering, moving lips. BW puts HIS hands on HER shoulder.)

BW

Kate, Kate, Kate, Kate—you surely ain't experienced no slowness of speech before, 'specially when you ridin' that pulpit of yours. What ya' think'd happen to those crowds of yours if they heard you fightin' for words in the pulpit? Now what, just what in the name of God did your mama tell you when you was a little girl? Spit it out, preacher girl!

KK

> (Softly, in a daze.)

. . . if you want something to leave you, don't pay it no mind. Don't pay it no mind.

BW

Don't pay what no mind?

KK

Don't pay it no mind.

BW

Don't pay what no mind?!

KK

    (Softly, still in a daze.)

I wanna go back to Denver, Mister Walters.

BW

That's out of the question, Misses Walters.

KK

Why can't I go back to Denver?

BW

Well, first of all, 'cause you're a married woman, that's why! And I say we're stayin' here in Iowa to start.

KK

But that's . . . that's where my people are.

BW

No, no siree, not anymore. I'm your people now, and I've been called to Iowa. You know that—called by the Lord to Iowa to sow the seed.

KK

    (Softly.)

I, I want to go back to Denver to sow the seed.

BW

Ain't gonna happen, Misses Walters. Ain't gonna happen. I'm the head of this new household and the Lord done called me to preach here in Iowa. Ain't hard to tell the difference between Iowa and Colorado. It was Iowa real plain. Heard it, heard it, heard it.

    (HIS hand raised, moving it across the imaginary wall in
    front of HIM with each syllable in I-O-WA.)

BW (cont'd)

I-O-WA. He said I-O-WA, I said, "Yes, Lord." He said, "I-O-WA." I said, "Yes, Lord."

KK

>(Softly, still stunned by the events and so in the habit of acquiescing.)

Yes, Lord.

BW

He said, "Marry her." I said, "Yes, Lord." He said, "Marry her."
I said,

>(HE looks at KK for the answer. PAUSE.)

BW (cont'd)

I said . . .

KK

>(Softer still.)

Yes, Lord.

BW

He said marry the lovely Kathryn, not Jill or Jane or any other
woman a God, no! He said, marry your sweet, lovely, sugar-thing,
Kate. And I said, yes Lord. Yes, Lord. Yes, Lord. Yep.

KK

>(Just mouthing.)

Yes, Lord.

BW

He said to me, you pay no mind to no first wife who choose to
abandon you and the cross and steal your boys from your preachin'
arms. You pay her no mind. No mind. Yep.

KK

>(Whispers.)

Yes, Lord.

BW

And you sure in heaven's name can't pay him no mind, whatever your crazy mom done gone and said. Yes, Lord.

KK

>(Softly.)

Yes, Lord.

>(BW looks at KK. PAUSE.)

KK (cont'd)

>(Louder.)

Yes, Lord.

BW

You gonna take off that coat now, Misses Walters?

>(HE starts to unbutton HER coat. SHE lets HIM, though not recognizing HIS presence.)

KK

>(Softly, almost a whisper at first.)

Yes, Lord.

>(HE continues unbuttoning HER coat. Succeeds, and takes it off. SHE does not respond, only . . .)

KK (cont'd)

Yes. Lord. Yes, Lord—

>(SHE continues through HIS exchange, intensifying with each.)

BW

Well, that's better, and don't you look mighty fine in your white weddin' gown. A sanctified, holy bride waitin' in purity for the bridegroom.

KK

(Continues to . . .)

Yes, Lord. Yes, Lord . . .

(SHE is working into an ecstatic frenzy, repeating with incremental intensity . . . as if calling down the Presence.)

KK (cont'd)

Yes, Lord.

(BW approaches HER. Watches, drawn . . . savoring possibility. HE reaches to take off the veil still covering HER face.)

KK (cont'd)

(Close to an altered state.)

Yes, Lord. Yes, Lord!

(Throughout.)

(HE lays HER veil neatly on the bed. Approaches HER, sees HER more entrenched stupor, HER head starting to shake back-and-forth.)

KK (cont'd)

Yes, Lord . . .

(HE grabs HER face with both HIS hands, stops HER shaking. SHE continues, building, screaming.)

KK (cont'd)

Yes, LORD!!

(HE pulls HER to HIMSELF, kisses HER.)

BW

(Pulling slightly away.)

Yes, Lord.

(KK is shaking HER head more violently, back-and-forth . . . SHE faints, crumbling to the floor. PAUSE. BW stares down at KK.)

BW (cont'd)

Now that's three times, Misses Kathryn Walters, three times in one night.

> (HE goes to the floor and tries to pull HER to HIMSELF, HER head held in HIS arms against HIS chest.)

BW (cont'd)

Well, my Kate, what we gonna do now?

> (HE kisses HER on the cheek. And gently lies HER on the floor.)

BW (cont'd)

Maybe you just need to get some more sleep. And that's alright, I guess.

> (HE sits on the edge of the bed, watches HER lying on the floor. HE takes off HIS tie and coat. PAUSE. HE begins to unbutton HIS shirt. Looks down at HER. PAUSE.)

BW (cont'd)

I do wish you'd not sleep too long.

> (HE takes off HIS shoes, throws them across the floor. HE grabs the empty glass and exits to the bathroom. PAUSE. HE enters with two glasses full of water. HE sits on the edge of the bed, holding both glasses of water, unsure. Begins drinking from one, downs the whole glass.)
>
> (HE sits on the floor next to KK. Places the glass of water in KK's unconscious hand, places HIS hand over HERS so as to raise the glass in a toast . . . Clicking the glasses.)

BW (cont'd)

To the newlyweds.

> (HE pauses, looking at HER.)

BW (cont'd)

And I'm sorry, darlin' to wake ya' up like this.

(HE then pours the water on HER face. SHE groans, coming out of it. Groggy.)

BW (cont'd)

What's got hold of you, bride?

(BW helps KK sit up, dries HER face with HIS handkerchief.)

BW (cont'd)

Ya' got that faintin' spell out? Now you tell me sweet thing that this faintin's all done. You silly bride.

KK

(Whispered, still slowly coming out of it.)

Again?

BW

What?

(PAUSE.)

KK

(Softly.)

I fainted again?

BW

Right after I kissed ya' again.

(PAUSE.)

KK

Like at the altar?

BW

Yep, you silly thing.

(PAUSE.)

KK

Don't kiss me for a while, all right?

BW

I'll do my best but can't be promising.

KK

Try, please.
>   (PAUSE.)

BW

On our weddin' night?

KK

Yes.

BW

Misses Burroughs Walters.
>   (KK is frozen.)

BW (cont'd)
>   (Leaning toward HER, playfully.)

Misses Burroughs Walters.
>   (Nothing.)

BW (cont'd)
>   (Rubbing HER shoulders.)

Misses Burroughs Walters, Misses Burroughs Walters, Misses
Burroughs Walters . . .
>   (HE repeats until KK slowly, stoically places hands over
>   HER ears. HE stops. Unbuttons the rest of HIS shirt.)

BW (cont'd)

I'll stop sayin' it then.
>   (PAUSE.)

BW (cont'd)

What else don't ya' wanna hear?
>   (SHE begins to drop HER hands from HER ears.)

BW (cont'd)

> (Seeing HER.)

Misses Burroughs Walters!

> (HER hands go back over ears.)

BW (cont'd)

> (Starting to find HIS preaching cadence.)

Guess it's kinda hard to take, is it? The new name there, new name written down in glory. Misses Burroughs Walters replacin' the Reverend Kathryn. I can see that old name bein' erased right now and replaced by the new name in that book of life. Old things passed away, darlin'. All things new. All things new. Yep.

> (PAUSE. Crosses to HER, nose to nose.)

BW (cont'd)

But my yoke's easy, darlin'. My burden's light.

> (Starts shouting—insulted, angered.)

Ya' hear me darlin', I ain't no hard cross to bear!!

> (Grabs at HER wrists to pull HER hands away from HER ears.)

BW (cont'd)

You listen to me!! My yoke's easy, my burden's light!!!

> (SHE breaks away, gets HER veil, runs to the other side of the room. HE does not pursue, only watches. SHE pulls HER veil over HER head while only snatching glimpses of HIM. HE goes to HIS suitcase, pulls out a liquor bottle, walks over to the end of the room, opposite KK. HE looks at the bottle, then at KK, smiles. HE takes a swig.)
>
> (PAUSE.)

KK

> (Lost, "what have I done?" Trembling.)

I . . . I'm sorry, Mister, Mister Wa-Walters—

BW

I guess then we're both sorry, aren't we?

> (PAUSE.)

KK

Is that liquor?

BW

It's my weddin' night, I can do anything I want. And besides, you never told me you was gonna act like someone I ain't never seen before, like some walkin' away polar bear.

> (BW takes a swig.)

KK

I'm sorry, Mister Walters.

BW

Sorry 'bout what?

KK

Sorry, sorry, I don't know what's got into me, but I started to feel a weight, a thousand-pound *weight* on me as soon as we left Colorado.

BW

What thousand-pound weight? I didn't feel no thousand-pound weight.

KK

And it only got bigger and bigger, and I don't know who it is or what it is, but it's big, Mister Walters, and it hasn't left.

BW

Well, there certainly wasn't any thousand-pound weight when you flew into my arms and put those lovely lips on mine before we left. What is it about the Colorado border that puts the freeze on my bride? A thousand-pound weight.

(BW takes another swig. KK taking it all in.)

KK

You never told me you drank liquor.

BW

Little wine for the stomach. Yep.

KK

I didn't know.

BW

What you think any man's gonna do on his weddin' night and his wife won't take nothing off?

KK

I . . . don't know, Mister Walters.

BW

What?

(Longer PAUSE.)

KK

(Not wanting to say this.)

And you never yelled at me like that before.

BW

I was in the spirit, preachin' with passion for my wife. What'd you expect?

KK

And you never grabbed me like that before.

BW

Ya' had ears and ya' needed to hear.

KK

And I never saw you drink before.

BW

You ain't been married before, darlin'.

KK

But . . . but you're an evangelist.

BW

And?

>   (PAUSE.)

KK

>   (Starting to find HER way)

I, I just didn't know.

BW

He who's forgiven much, loves much, sweetheart. And besides, marital bliss includes knowin' intimate things about the bridegroom that are off-limits to the public. I call 'em "holy secrets." Yep.

KK

So, you've done it enough to give it a name?

>   (BW takes another swig.)

BW

I guess.

KK

Holy secrets.

BW

All things are lawful.

>   (PAUSE.)

KK

But the Book also says not all things are expedient.

BW

All things are lawful.

KK

But the Book says not to be controlled by anything.

BW

Food for the stomach and the stomach for food.

KK

And God will destroy them both.

BW

    (Laughs.)
I fell in love with a preacher who thinks she knows more Bible than me.

KK

Don't know about that.

BW

About my fallin' in love or you're knowin' more Bible than me?

KK

Tell the truth, you probably forgot more than I know.

BW

Don't know about that.

KK

What have I done, Mister Walters?

BW

Gone and got yourself married, Misses Walters.
    (PAUSE.)

KK

You were the finest preacher I ever heard. I love to hear you preach, Mister Walters.

BW

(Offering bottle.)

Want some?

KK

No.

BW

C'mon, it'll loosen ya' up.

KK

Don't need to loosen up.

BW

Ya' drink from the living waters, is that it?

KK

So do you, Mister Walters.

BW

Yep. It's the reason we're equally yoked. Even though you got this thousand-pound weight that suddenly invites you to keep faintin' at the drop of a hat.

> (PAUSE. BW takes another sip, puts the cap back on the bottle and puts it back in HIS suitcase. Begins to unpack suitcase and place items in room chest of drawers.)

BW (cont'd)

Don't think anybody ever saw me before.

KK

Your first wife never saw you drink liquor?

BW

Why would ya' wanna bring her up now?

KK

I guess I'm just wondering.

BW

She was usually too drunk to notice.

    (PAUSE.)

BW (cont'd)

And my little boys had to put her to bed.

KK

Why didn't you?

    (PAUSE.)

KK (cont'd)

Why?

BW

Revival somewhere, I suppose.

KK

Is that why she left you?

BW

Partly.

KK

But . . . I remember meeting her and the boys when you first came to my church. She seemed devoted to you and to the Lord.

BW

She was on the wagon. She promised she'd stop.

KK

And she broke her promise.

BW

And the second time I came to Denver she'd already abandoned the ministry and taken my two boys.

(PAUSE.)

KK

Mister Walters, why'd you let her take 'em? How can a woman drunk take care of two boys?

BW

They left while I was away. Lawyer said I wouldn't have a chance gettin' 'em from her since I was always gone myself and it'd be her word against mine.

KK

What would be her word against yours?

(PAUSE.)

BW

Her accusations, my accusations.

(PAUSE.)

KK

Can I ask you something, Mister Walters?

BW

Fire away, there darlin'. Maybe this will lighten the weight that's possessing ya.

(PAUSE.)

KK

(Turns to BW.)

What were her accusations?

BW

Why would you wanna know?

KK

Cause I realize I married you, and I know I love you more than any other man, ever. And no man's ever been kinder or sweeter and I never felt more loved and secure than when I'm in your arms, and I do love you, Mister Walters—

BW

But ya' don't know me all that well, is that it?

KK

(Near tears.)

I'm sorry, Mister Walters. I'm so sorry.

BW

She accused me of all the things normal for a wife to accuse an itinerate evangelist: Too much time away from home, too much time in other people's homes. Too much focus on the others. But that's no surprise to you, young female evangelist who used to own the hearts of all the elect in Colorado.

KK

I didn't know.

BW

Well, now ya' do.

(PAUSE.)

BW (cont'd)

You gonna remove that veil so I can see your face or am I gonna have to guess how your beauty shines?

KK

(Looks down.)

I'm not beautiful, Mister Walters.

BW

How in heaven's name can a new bride still in her weddin' gown say she ain't beautiful?

KK

Betty Grable . . . Betty Grable's beautiful. I'm not. But I try.

BW

You don't have to try very hard; I'll tell ya that's the heaven's truth.

KK

That's awfully nice of you, Mister Walters, but I never thought so. I remember as a little girl wishing I was beautiful but gave up on that once I looked in the mirror for an hour straight hoping for a miracle and realizing it wasn't going to happen.

BW

Now why ya' unveilin' such things nobody need to know?

    (PAUSE.)

KK

I'm hoping you need to know, I guess.

BW

One hour straight lookin' in the mirror waitin' for the miracle that you think never came.

KK

Yes.

BW

So, you decide to pay that kind of outward beauty no mind. You want it to walk away and haunt some other lonely soul, so you don't pay it any mind, just like your mother said. And ya' end up beautiful to me anyway and in every way. Aww, but the truth is you was always probably too busy thinking 'bout heavenly things.

    (PAUSE.)

KK

Don't know about that. But I will say I did think you were the most handsome man I'd ever met.

BW

Well, it seems like you changed your opinion.

> (PAUSE.)

KK

No, I didn't, Mister Walters.

BW

Well, you got a funny way of makin' me feel handsome.

KK

Nothing's changed. You still are.

BW

Tell me that without a veil over your face, Misses Walters.

KK

I'm not ready yet, Mister Walters.

> (PAUSE.)

BW

Are you gonna let me know when you're ready or am I gonna have to keep hopin' 'til Jesus comes?

KK

I'm sorry. I—

BW

'Bout what? Gettin' married to the most handsome man ya' ever met?

> (PAUSE.)

KK

I don't mean to be stubborn, but I—

BW

So, you're sorry 'bout bein' "stubborn"? Naw, I don't think you're stubborn, I just think you're scared a bit—yep, that's it. You're just afraid.

KK

I am afraid, Mister Walters.

BW

Yep. Marriage is a frightenin' thing sometimes if ya' let it scare ya'. And ya' can't let it scare ya'. Ya' gotta take that demon a fear and cast it out of yourself. And the best thing to do, the best act of faith to defeat your fear would be to take off your veil as a start.

(PAUSE. KK does not move.)

BW (cont'd)

(Again, finding preaching cadence.)

D'ya think David had no fear when he slew Goliath? Of course, he was afraid, but in faith he went to the brook and gathered the five smooth stones. Still afraid, but in faith put them in his sling and in faith let those stones of his fly toward the head of the beast.

(PAUSE.)

BW (cont'd)

Now you gotta slay that beast!

(PAUSE. KK doesn't move.)

BW (cont'd)

Well?

KK

I've never loved anyone more than you, Mister Walters.

BW

Ya' got a funny way a showin' it this evening.

KK

I apologize. I'm just—

BW

Like ah said, you're scared, that's all. But remember perfect love casts out fear.

KK

Then mine's not a perfect love.

BW

So, me not havin' no fear means mine is?

KK

Maybe you have more confidence, more faith that this is the will of God.

BW

Woman, how could there be any doubt of that? You see me, I'm already done unpackin' all my clothes for our honeymoon. Old things have passed away, I'm ready for my journey with you in the light of the Lord! Now when you gonna take any step of faith in this?

    (PAUSE.)

KK

Did you have any fear in your first marriage, Mister Walters?

BW

I believe fear's an insult to the sovereignty of God, Misses Walters!

KK

So, you were not afraid?

BW

No.

KK

How about when your boys were born?

BW

No.

KK

How about when she started drinking?

BW

I had confidence God would deliver her.

KK

Evidently, he didn't.

BW

Not true—he's deliverin' and will continue to deliver.

KK

Through someone other than you?

BW

Our God works in mysterious ways, mysterious ways. Now are you gonna take something off and loosen up a little?

KK

I didn't know any of this. Why didn't you tell me?

BW

No need to tell ya'. What good would that do?

KK

But you were her husband, supposed to serve her like Christ served the church.

(PAUSE.)

BW

I don't suppose the Church was ever alcoholic. And on top of that, I don't suppose I'm Jesus.

KK

So, you weren't afraid?

BW

Nope.

KK

Was she afraid?

BW

Ain't it obvious, any person drownin' in drink is afraid of nearly everything. And it made those two boys terribly afraid. Made me angry and sick to see her always fearin' the worst of everything. Let me tell you, I wasn't gonna live in no Egypt of ignorance and fear. I was gonna walk through the Red Sea of opportunity and wander in a wilderness demanding the courage to expose myself to the refining fires of God.

    (PAUSE.)

KK

So, she never crossed the Red Sea.

BW

It's like she's dead in some Egyptian tomb. What does livin' faith have to do with that? To be wedded to despair is to die a thousand deaths every day. I was called to walk in faith amongst the living and let the dead bury the dead.

    (PAUSE.)

KK

    (Not accusatory, softly.)

Your two little boys aren't part of the living?

BW

What is this, an interrogation? Why didn't you show no signs of this before? Questionin' my release from an Egyptian bondage.

KK

So, your first wife was an alcoholic when you married her?

BW

I have a good mind to—

> (BW crosses back to the dresser, pulls out the drawer.)

BW (cont'd)

I'm sensing that maybe I oughta just start packin' these clothes back here in this suitcase seein' you are in no mind to do nothin' but interrogate me. I'd rather ya' did what your mommy said when you want something to go away—paying someone no mind's better than questioning 'em like a drunk-on-dominatin' prosecutor. Ya' reminded me of your mother's wisdom before—when you had criticism from disgruntled folk, when ya' had some pilgrim angry 'cause he wasn't healed immediately and he was hounding ya', blamin' you for his lack of faith. And you would go on in some Missouri-honed tranquility, payin' it no mind. Ya' continued to march on unaffected. And is this what you're gonna do with me? March back to Denver unaffected by my love? And all of it only after ya' push my mind and body through some interrogation wringer? Is this what my wedding night's come to?

KK

I'm sorry, Mister Walters. But I'm such a fool for not asking this before.

BW

Now why would ya' be such a fool? Cause maybe ya' wouldn't have married me if you knew the truth? Well, that's maybe what getting married is—only some kind of confirmation that we're all fools for Christ anyway.

KK

I don't know—

BW

Well, I'm telling you the truth and I'll keep telling you the truth, and the truth will set ya' free, 'cause God knows you need to be set free tonight!

KK

I'm sorry, Mister Walters, I'm sure I've put you in a bad way.

BW

Fire away, ask anything ya' want if ya' think it'll help. Ask me if I ever made a pack with the devil, or if I ever was a moon shiner or was ever a Congregationalist or Shriner!! Go ahead fire away.

    (PAUSE.)

KK

Did ya' love her when ya' first married her knowin' that she drank?

BW

Course I loved her, and she wasn't drinkin' all that much when we first married.

KK

So, what drove her to—

BW

She didn't drink at all when we first met and got married, not at all!

KK

So, was it the marriage that drove her to alcohol?

    (BW starts putting clothes in HIS suitcase.)

BW

Naaa, wasn't the marriage—and I'm really gettin' aggravated by your interrogatin'!

KK

I don't mean—

BW

You don't mean, what?!

KK

I sure don't mean to be aggravating. I'm just confused by a—

BW

Confused? You're supposed to be my wife, so what's so confusin' 'bout that?

KK

I just—

BW

What's so confusin' 'bout walkin' in simple faith in a marriage blessed by God? It ain't complicated, Miss Kathryn.

KK

It would just help me, I think, if I knew—

BW

Knew what? What? You're looking for clarity a little late. Nothin's completely clear. We're all looking in a glass darkly! Faith is the absence of things hoped for, the evidence of things not seen!! You know that! This is a walk of faith.

    (PAUSE.)

KK

I'm just very scared, Mister Walters. Maybe I shouldn't have said that I'd marry you.

BW

You sure got a great way of insultin' a man.

KK

I'm sorry, I don't mean to be insulting. I'm just afraid. I'm afraid of—of loving you more than I love God. I'm sorry, Mister Walters.

BW

Like I said, this is a walk of faith.

KK

I'm afraid my flock in Denver won't understand.

BW

This is a walk of faith.

KK

I'm afraid our love for each other won't be enough.

BW

This is a walk of faith!

KK

And that one day you might get tired of my ordinary looks.

BW

This is about faith! Faith!! Don't you see?!!

(PAUSE.)

KK

And I'm afraid of being naked in front of you.

(PAUSE.)

BW

(Quietly.)

Even that might be a walk of faith, Misses Walters.

(Long PAUSE.)

KK

Did you know, Mister Walters, that this was my momma's wedding dress? It's one of the few things I took after she died. My daddy always told me how beautiful she looked in it. The veil's new, though. I bought it when you first asked me to marry, and I had one day to find it, didn't I? My momma kept her veil, said that each woman requires her own. She said that makes the lifting of the veil that much more holy. So, when she died it was the only thing I took, though I felt silly, thinking I'd never marry on account of my being married to the Lord, and on account of my being so ordinary. And to lift the veil, well that's the start in my heart of the revelation.

BW

The revelation?

KK

A face revealed that says, "You can know me, at least anything that's worth knowing about me." What was hidden is hidden no longer. And though I'd shown you my face before, and let you kiss me, lifting the veil is an invitation beyond the time and space of a kiss. It's beyond the heart pounding of awakened passion, Mister Walters, which, of course, you've awakened in me. It's letting you, no, it's asking you to have full access to my soul.

BW

And I've said I'll take full access to your soul and likewise.

KK

But it's another threshold, isn't it?

BW

Already carried ya' over one, unconscious though you were.

KK

And maybe—I'm sorry, Mister Walters—I'd rather be unconscious crossing the next one.

BW

I already woke ya' up three times tonight.

KK

And maybe we're two preachers used to not opening up much to anyone else, especially our flocks.

BW

Itinerant preachers don't have no flock.

(PAUSE.)

KK

I'm trying to figure out why I came with you, left everything I knew, every authority I had to be swallowed up in your authority. I never loved anyone like you, Mister Walters. You've taken me to a trembling place of submission before I ever knew what came over me. And then I came to that altar, invited to repeat those vows and I got swept away into what I hope was a holy unconsciousness. I'm terribly afraid, Mister Walters. I rushed into this.

BW

And you want to be swept away again, swept away from here, swept away from me, like I'm some forgotten piece a dust?

KK

No, I—

BW

Why can't we get back to talkin' 'bout "full access" to each other's souls?

KK

Because I'm afraid to think about how much I love you, Mister Walters, because I'm afraid that I'm too good at keeping anyone from full access to my soul. I've come to the conclusion—as much as this is embarrassing to say—that preaching is one of my ways of keeping people from knowing my own soul. I come on so fiery asking the flock about their souls, they're unable to ask me about mine. And I think I've come to like that arrangement too much.

BW

Why should they know all about your soul? That's what God's for.

KK

Maybe so, but I'm standing here like a lost lamb, fearing I've wandered too far away. I know next to nothing about this wilderness, Mister Walters.

    (PAUSE.)

BW

Maybe I'm God's instrument for your wilderness, your "cloud by day" and your "fire by night"?

KK

I don't know, Mister Walters.

BW

    (Realizing, painfully.)
And maybe *I'm* the wilderness. Ain't that a sorry thought.

KK

I don't know.

BW

So, what do you know, Miss Kathryn?

KK

That I love you, Mister Walters, maybe too much; that I love God and that I'm a lost lamb who's used to being the shepherd.

BW

And I'm the unfamiliar terrain, the bona fide, ain't-no-oasis-in-sight, wilderness? That's it, ain't it, Miss Kathryn?

KK

It's true I don't know you very well. I did so foolishly rush into this. I'm sorry, Mister—

BW

Well then, let's start now! What else ya' need to know 'bout this "wilderness"?

KK

Mister Walters, I'm—

BW

What else? Whatever you need to find to be that "cloud by day" and that "fire by night" to walk through this land of "deserts and of pits," this land of "drought, and of the shadow of death," this wilderness called the Reverend Burroughs A. Walters?!

(PAUSE.)

KK

Maybe that's it. Maybe there's just so much I don't know.

BW

Fire away. What else you need to know 'bout me? I want to give ya' full access to my soul!

(KK is hesitant.)

BW (cont'd)
Go ahead! Fire away!!

KK

So . . . so, Jessie's got your boys?

BW

How'd you know her name? I never told you her name, did I?

KK

Of course, we met the first time I invited you to come preach at my church in Denver.

BW

And you met my little boys.

KK

Sweet boys they were.

BW

And she took 'em and left me to preach alone. And I decided to never mention her name aloud again!

KK

And since then, I've never heard you say her name.

BW

And I did that for a reason.

KK

Yes, Mister Walters.

BW

For a reason, an important reason. But you already knew.

KK

     (Softly.)

Yes.

BW

I never said it cause that name would possess me with a spirit of melancholy and darkness.

KK

Her name would do that?

BW

Still does and don't say it again. Don't say that name.

KK

I figured you didn't say her name as a courtesy to me, not wanting to make me feel compared.

(PAUSE.)

BW

That too.

KK

We met that first time you came through. She seemed awfully nice to me, and those boys were darling. And I do remember now that you didn't introduce me that first time we met. It was just her and me and your little boys. And to you it was like they weren't even there. And she came up after sitting there in the sanctuary for some time and introduced herself to me. She seemed awfully nice. The boys were too bashful to say their names. Awfully cute those little Walters boys were.

(PAUSE. HE sits on the bed, lets out a huge sigh.)

BW

Yeh. Miss Kathryn, maybe you're right. Maybe you should keep that veil over that sweet head of yours as long as you need. Maybe you need to just stand there waitin' for a bolt of light to show ya' the way through this sudden wilderness. And maybe I need to be more patient like the farmer waitin' patiently for the autumn and spring rains. Maybe it takes more time than this night holds.

(PAUSE. Suddenly KK turns and announces.)

KK

I need to go back.

(SHE walks toward HER coat.)

KK (cont'd)

I need to get that coat and get back to Denver and that's what—

BW

What? You can't go back to Denver; you're married to a man who's been called to Iowa.

KK

Maybe I've been called back to Denver!

BW

Don't work that way, Miss Kathryn. And besides, you ain't leavin' now no how. It's working its way to midnight and those October winds ain't gonna get nothing but colder.

(KK lunges for HER coat that BW has now blocked.)

KK

Let me have my coat! I'm leaving for Denver and returning to my flock!

BW

You ain't leavin' me, Miss Kathryn; I simply forbid it! You gotta remember who's head of this marriage!

KK

And how can you forbid something I've been told to do!? Maybe I was a fool coming here, but I'm sure not a fool going back.

BW

Leavin' me alone here when the call's to Iowa?

KK

I'm going to ask you again, Mister Walters, to give me my coat please.

BW

And be an accomplice to your foolishness? Why do ya' need a coat? If the Lord's telling you to return to Denver than what's a little ol'

coat for keeping ya' warm? Why, you should be fine in the warmth
of *God's* glory!

>   (KK stares at BW. HE folds HER coat over HIS crossed
>   arms. KK then crosses for HER suitcase.)

KK

Then I'll just get my suitcase here—

>   (BW lunges in front of HER, blocks HER path to the
>   suitcase.)

BW

I think if you're so sure this is of God, then go out in real faith like
Jesus said to the twelve to take no bag for the journey.

>   (SHE turns and exits quickly.)

BW (cont'd)

And the bride returns to Egypt without a word. And the wrath of
God lets her.

>   (BW freezes, still processing HER departure. After a
>   PAUSE, HE sits on the edge of the bed.)

BW (cont'd)

She ain't goin' nowhere.

>   (PAUSE.)

BW (cont'd)

She ain't goin' nowhere. She loves me, she does.

>   (PAUSE.)

BW (cont'd)

And the wrath a God'll let her go for a while. But she ain't goin'
nowhere . . . She ain't.

>   (HE holds HER coat a little tighter.)

BW (cont'd)

She ain't.

END OF ACT ONE

Act Two

TIME: Ten minutes later

> (KK enters. HER veil remains over HER face. SHE looks
> longingly at HIM, torn; is it to get "one last look"? BW is
> sitting on the edge of the bed, back to the door.)

KK

Mister Walters, it's gotten warmer outside. I really don't need
my coat.

BW

You came back to tell me that?

KK

You said if God's calling me back to Denver, I don't need no coat to
keep me warm. And I don't need my coat. And if God's called me
back to Denver, I don't need anything in that suitcase.

BW

Some kinda fleece mentionin' to your soul that it's alright to leave
your husband of a few hours?

KK

But I'm asking you to let me take one thing. Don't worry, I'm not
taking this suitcase.

> (KK crosses to get HER luggage. Begins to
> rummage through.)

KK (cont'd)

I'm being sent out to return to my first love. With power and authority over all demons, and to cure diseases. I'm to take nothing for the journey, neither staff, nor bag, neither bread nor money. And I don't need two coats . . . I don't need even one coat.

(SHE finds HER toothbrush.)

KK (cont'd)

I'm only taking this on my reconciliation journey as the Bride of Christ.

BW

Your toothbrush? So, the Lord can keep you safe and warm in that weddin' gown, but he can't keep your teeth clean?

KK

Okay, maybe it's his will I should fast.

(SHE holds up the toothbrush.)

KK (cont'd)

But just in case, I'm bringing it. No place in Scripture says I can't carry a toothbrush. And no place in Scripture that says it isn't proper for a woman of God to want to feel she's sleeping on her pilgrim journey back to the fold with clean teeth.

BW

No place in Scripture says you should leave your husband on your wedding night.

KK

Good-bye, Mister Walters. I fear I've made a mistake.

(SHE begins to exit. BW runs to HER, grabs HER, wraps both arms around HER.)

BW

Ain't no mistakes according to the sovereign will of God. You can't go, Miss Kathryn. I'm forbiddin' ya' to go!

KK

Mister Walters, let go of me!

BW

You're my wife in the eyes a God and ya' ain't gonna leave!

KK

(Struggling to free HERSELF.)

Let go of me!

BW

Miss Kate, I'm not gonna let ya' go. I'm wantin' ya' to hear me just one more time.

KK

(Struggling still.)

Let go of me!!

BW

I'll let ya' go but ya' gotta promise before ya' do that you'll hear me one more time.

KK

(The largest attempt to free HERSELF.)

Let me go!!

BW

(Gripping tighter.)

It's no use Miss Kathryn, I'm not lettin' go 'til you promise me you're gonna listen to me.

(SHE continues to struggle.)

BW (cont'd)

I'm sorry to say, but I like a fight in a woman. And you ain't gonna win this one. Now I'm not lettin' go 'til you listen.

(SHE lets out an anguished cry/scream.)

BW (cont'd)
Now I ain't gonna tell ya' how pretty ya' look with that determined face not hid by no veil. But ya' are a pretty thing.

> (SHE is giving up HER struggle.)

BW (cont'd)
Now that's better.

> (SHE looks off, it's no use.)

BW (cont'd)
That's better. Just relax. I ain't gonna keep ya' in no prison. For if the Son has set ya' free, you're free indeed.

KK

> (Resigned.)

. . . indeed.

BW

> (Still holding on.)

And besides, you just run off in the night, this boy'll come searchin' for ya', houndin' ya'. Lookin' with an unceasing love. That's right, Miss Kate. Like some Gomer runnin' away, always runnin' away from the place that knows ya' and loves ya'.

KK
You said you'd let me go if I listened.

BW
Yep, I did.

> (PAUSE.)

KK
I'm listening.

BW
I'm waitin' for the struggle to be gone from your arms, your legs . . . you're boltin' to get free.

KK

> (Releasing.)

Okay, it's gone.

BW

You sure, cause I'm still feelin' it.

KK

It's gone, as much as I know it to be gone. Now let me go.

BW

You ain't gonna run off?

KK

No.

BW

You promise over a stack a Bibles?

KK

Yes.

BW

And you let your yes be yes, and your no be no. Don't need no stack a Bibles, do ya'?

KK

I'm listening, Mister Walters.

> (PAUSE. HE slowly loosens HIS grip, waiting with each incremental movement of unfastening to see assurances that SHE is not perched to flee. Finally assured, HE quickly finds a chair and places it in front of HER.)

BW

Now if you're really gonna listen, ya' need to sit down.

> (SHE does. PAUSE.)

KK

I've sat down, Mister Walters.

BW

Yeh.

KK

So, what do you want me to listen to before I head back to my flock?

BW

So, you're still talkin' about a "flock"?

KK

Shouldn't I be?

BW

Seems to me that my Bible tells me something 'bout a man leavin' his mother and a woman leavin' her home and the two becomin' one flesh. Don't say nothing 'bout a "flock."

KK

Is this what I was sitting down to listen to?

BW

Don't think so but doesn't mean ya' shouldn't.

KK

So please tell me what I'm supposed to hear so I can ponder it on the way back to Denver.

BW

Without a coat.

KK

I told you, the Lord has already provided the necessary warmth.

BW

Guess you don't need any coat in hell either now do ya'?

KK

So now I'm going to hell?

BW

Didn't say that in any way, shape, or form. Just makin' a factual statement that you don't need no coat in hell.

KK

Nor in heaven, I would think.

BW

Well, ain't that the truth.

KK

You said you'd let me go if I listened to what you were going to say. You being a man of God, I expect you to tell me what you think I need to hear, then let me be free to leave.

BW

Free? Of course, you're free. Nobody seen me put a gun to your head to marry me. You did it of your own free will.

KK

Yes. That's true, Mister Walters. I love you; never loved another man like I love you. But—

BW

But that ain't enough? Is that right?

    (Getting worked up again.)

You made a vow before God, and I suppose that ain't enough?! You not only proclaiming your love for me but vowing to be true before the throne of heaven and ten thousand angels!!

    (KK rises from HER seat. Starts to exit.)

BW (cont'd)

(Catches HIMSELF.)

Oops, that's right. Need to try to calm down, 'cause I got something ya' gotta hear.

(SHE stops, still standing.)

KK

Now I know you don't have anything to say before I leave.

BW

Please, don't go.

KK

Is that what you need me to hear? 'Cause that I'll believe is from your heart, but not anything about ten thousand angels hearing my vows—

BW

What about it?

KK

Mister Walters, sorry to say, but there weren't ten thousand angels witnessing our secret wedding. And there weren't but a few people witnessing my fainting during the ceremony.

BW

But those vows meant something to me, and they meant something to God.

KK

What about the ten thousand angels?

BW

Well, maybe not ten thousand, but they did mean something to the heavenly witnesses.

KK

And are the heavenly witnesses watching us right now?

BW

Kate, you know the answer to that.

KK

And did they see you take a drink of that liquor?

BW

Psalm 139 declares that there's nowhere a man can hide from the hound of heaven.

KK

So at least it wasn't ten thousand angels taking the time to spectate.

BW

Miss Kate, I'll admit I wax with hyperbolic eloquence on occasion. But on the other hand, who's to say there wasn't a million heavenly witnesses—

KK

Mister Walters—

BW

        (Interrupting.)

But, Miss Kathryn, that ain't the point I'm trying to make, and the point I'm trying to make is that human vows *before* God may as well be made directly *to* God for all the seriousness the Almighty takes 'em. Our Lord said in his Sermon on the Mount that we should not break our vows.

KK

And I made a vow to my flock to be a shepherd for them. And how I keep that vow is by running off in secret and making a vow to you. And God heard them both.

        (PAUSE.)

KK (cont'd)

And you really didn't have one more thing to say while you had me sitting down, did you?

BW

I did. And it could've been a billion angels.

KK

I suppose it could have been a trillion.

BW

Nothin's impossible with God. And I think I know what you should be hearin' before you go.

KK

So, what are you waiting for?

>   (PAUSE.)

BW

Do ya' think you'd faint again if I kissed ya'?

KK

Don't want to find out right now, Mister Walters.

BW

I promise I wouldn't wake ya' up, I'd just let ya' sleep 'til the snoring done died.

KK

I suppose then you'd, what?

BW

Thank God ya' stayed with me at least one night, Misses Walters.

KK

Don't say that, please.

BW

Alright then. What d'ya want me to call ya, Kate my bride? And before ya' answer that, please answer me one question before ya' run back to Denver cause the Lord told ya' to. Do you love me?

KK

Yes, I do Mister Walters.

BW

But that really ain't the question, the one question I'm fixin' to ask.

KK

It isn't? So, what I'm supposed to hear before I go is something you're going to ask me and it isn't about whether or not I love you?

BW

No, but here it is—it's this right here, let me make sure I phrase it right. Let me put it this way, now—I say the Lord told me to marry ya' and bring ya' to start the ministry here in Iowa. Is that right?

KK

Right.

BW

And you say the Lord's now telling you to return to Denver and tend to your old flock even though ya' just testified before God, two witnesses, a justice-of-the-peace, and let's not argue over how many angels, about being faithful in sickness and in health for richer or for poorer. Am I right?

KK

Right.

BW

How could we both be right, Misses Walters?

KK

We both can't be right, I suppose.

BW

No, we both can't be right. So, who's wrong?

KK

Mister Walters, I don't know that I care at this point. I just want to—

BW

Now hold on there a minute, I'm not finished. So, who's wrong? And let's just say I mean that in a rhetorical way.

    (PAUSE.)

KK

Mister Walters, I'm not confident I was right in running off with you to get married and leaving the church in Denver.

BW

So, why'd ya' do it?

KK

I don't know now. I loved you more than any other man I ever met. And when you had me in your arms, I felt that's where I belonged. And when I sat under your pulpit preaching, I sensed the power of the Spirit, mesmerized by the presence of God. And you asked me and I couldn't say anything but "yes" there in that moment . . . and it was that moment that struck my heart and gouged its way into my soul and seemed to set for me a new course. And then came the weight, the heavy weight that wouldn't let me breathe and asks me to doubt whether one passing moment of weakness should dictate the rest of my life. I talked to no one about your proposal. I should have brought it up in the church, the church that I loved—one of the elders should have known. I told no one and that was wrong, Mister Walters.

BW

It was between me and you and the Lord.

KK

And I prayed, I did. Then I followed you as in a trance—

BW

A love trance, allowed by the Lord.

KK

I put on this dress and adjusted this veil and then the weight came . . . and it wouldn't let me breathe.

BW

Ya' sure breathin' fine now.

KK

Denver will let me breathe again, and I'll be wed to my flock again . . . I'll ask them to forgive me for this betrayal. And they'll forgive me.

BW

Betrayal?! Ya' still love me, don't ya', Kate?

KK

I've told you I do, but I don't think that matters now.

BW

Of course, it matters—love bears all things, endures all things, hopes all things, believes all things. So how does the thought of you leaving me line up with Scripture? Love even covers over a multitude of sins, maybe even what you might call your "mistake" of leavin' Denver and comin' with me.

KK

Mister Walters, have you told me the one thing you wanted to say before I left, that one thing I needed to be seated to hear?

BW

Not sure, and I may need to wait on it for some confirmation.

KK

Wait on what, Mister Walters?

BW

Haven't you said already that I was the most handsome man ya' ever met?

KK

Please tell me the—

BW

And haven't you said already that I was the best preacher ya' ever met?

KK

I'm going back to Denver.

> (SHE gets up, but this time heads to HER luggage. HE follows HER.)

KK (cont'd)

And I've decided to take my luggage—

BW

Just one night, I promise I won't touch ya' if that's the way it is. I'm a gentleman, I won't force my way back into your heart.

KK

Excuse me, Mister Walters—

BW

You can, and I swear this on a stack of Gideon Bibles—and there must be one in here—that you can go to bed, sleep your dream, and leave what you might think is a nightmare, and I'll just stay up, look out at the stars, pray, and look at my one-night bride.

KK

And be awfully crabby in the morning from getting no sleep and from watching me leave. It's best I go now, Mister Walters. The Lord will take care of me.

BW

The Lord will take care of you? How do you know? It's nighttime, Miss Kathryn, no telling what's out there—

KK

(Interrupting.)

Mister Walters, I—

BW

How do you know the Lord's gonna take care of you? Leavin' your husband on your wedding night, launchin' out into the darkness—

KK

I have faith, Mister Walters—

BW

And I have more faith that we can work this out, whatever this thing to be worked out is!

KK

I have faith that I can walk in the valley of the shadow of death and live in resurrection life!

BW

I think you're temptin' the Lord, that's what you're doin', tempting the Lord!

KK

Mister Walters, I would like to get my luggage.

(PAUSE. BW steps aside.)

BW

Okay, then, get your luggage, but you're temptin' the Lord.

> (KK starts to close HER luggage, gather what BW has strewn across the bed— nightgown, etc.)

KK

Mister Walters, and I say this respectfully on account of never hearing a more Spirit-filled preacher in my pulpit, but I don't think you know what tempting the Lord really is, because I'll be honest with you, I don't, and I don't want to know and please . . .

> (Everything is gathered.)

KK (cont'd)

Let me go, I'm sorry, but I'm going back.

> (BW falls to HIS knees.)

BW

> (Getting louder with each sentence.)

I got too much pride to stand in your way, allow you to do something that's gonna kill me, but, as you see it, be the next best thing to godliness for you. It's gonna kill me but make you more pleasing to the Lord. How in the name of God—just think about what this is gonna do to me, being abandoned by two wives. Two wives . . .

> (Starting to cry, then wails *loudly*.)

Two wives, O Lord, let this pass from me and bring her back, bring her back. I have the faith, dear Lord, I have the faith that my beloved wife, Kate, will be blocked by your angels from leavin' that door and into the darkness. This is not by my power, not by my might, but by your Spirit, O Lord!

KK

> (Angrily, as loud as BW.)

Don't tell me that your faith rests on whether angels permit me to leave this room?!

BW

> (Loudest yet.)

Thank you, Lord, she stopped to say something before her uncrossin' the threshold!!

KK

I already "uncrossed" it, without a coat, or did you forget?

BW

Prevent her, Lord, from uncrossin' the threshold!!

KK

This threshold you carried me over when I was unconscious just might be the Red Sea that my God is going to part for me to walk through!!

BW

> (Louder.)

If that is the Red Sea, Lord, let me be the Pharaoh of your righteousness, keeping my young bride—

KK

> (Screams.)

I'm not a young bride, Mister Walters!!!

BW

Keepin' my young bride from the wilderness of doublemindedness! Keep her from the wilderness of doublemindedness!! Lord, show her there is no night fire in the sky to lead her through the wilderness of doublemindedness, none whatso—

KK

> (Interrupting.)

You're not talking to God, you're talking to me, aren't you?!

BW

Lord, help my bride, like you help your bride!!

KK

Talk to me all you want in that posture of prayer, but I'm walking through that door and getting back to my flock. I'm sorry, Mister Walters, but I've made a mistake!

> (KK starts to exit, suddenly stops when SHE hears a pounding on the motel door.)

BW

> (Still on knees.)

O Lord, I hear your knockin'. Let us trust your servant at that door!

KK

Mister Walters, you have no idea who's on the other side of that door.

BW

> (Still on knees.)

Behold, someone stands at the door and knocks—

> (KK goes to the door. The MOTEL MANAGER'S voice is heard.)

MM

> (Loud whisper.)

You folks know what time it is?

KK

We are so sorry, we—

MM

I could hear your two's voices over in my office, but even if I couldn't I got two folks in the last-minute complaining 'bout the noise over here—

BW

We're sorry, but we got in a little late on account of it being our weddin' night.

MM

One from a couple with two little babies been cryin' all night before you got here and they finally gets 'em settled and you two come and unsettle 'em.

> (PAUSE. The MM sizes up the situation, KK in HER wedding dress, with suitcase in hand.)

MM (cont'd)

Looks like she's changed her mind.

KK

I have changed—

BW

> (Loud, forgets, then corrects.)

Only in her—oops, sorry, forgot about the little ones—

> (Loud whisper.)

Only in her mind she changed, but her spirit hasn't changed.

KK

I've changed my mind and fear I've made a dreadful mistake and sense the Spirit's telling me to leave.

MM

All I'm asking is that you don't let the whole world in on your little spat about Lord-knows-what.

BW

It's not a little spat and the good Lord sure knows what it's about—

MM

I'm just asking—

BW

I know what you're askin'—

> (Falls again to HIS knees.)

BW (cont'd)
Lord, all I'm askin' is for you to tell me why, WHY would ya' bring
your bride—

MM
Sir, I'm gonna have to ask you again to quiet down or—

BW
(Quieter.)
Why would ya' lead your servant to a precipice and then—

MM
Your prayers are still too loud when people are trying to sleep. Now
if you can't—

BW
(Quieter still, quickly seeks MM's okay.)
Allow the bride to jump off into the night of broken promises and
leave her lord alone in despair.

MM
(To KK.)
Make sure he keeps his praying at that volume tonight.

KK
Since I'm leaving, I can't promise anything about him and
his prayers.

MM
So, you're leaving him tonight?

KK
Yes.

MM
Right now?

KK

Yes.

MM

Where you going?

KK

Back to Denver.

MM

Denver? This late at night? How ya' getting to Denver?

KK

Don't know. I'll trust the Lord for a way.

BW

(Still on knees.)

O Lord, how can you honor her trust in you in this way? I only ask that you honor my trust in you, that she'll see the error of her way and stay.

MM

Sir, keep the volume on your prayers down. I'm asking you as a Christian myself to make it a silent prayer for the sake of your neighbors.

BW

(Still on knees.)

O Lord, I can't be silent when my soul's afire, but allow our neighbors to sleep soundly despite the tumult of the newlyweds—

MM

Sir, if you don't quiet down, I'm gonna have to call the Sheriff—

BW

(Persisting, more fervently.)

Let the little boys be touched by your providing hand of comfort,

let their mother be comforted, unperturbed by the disturbance in
my soul!

MM

Okay, that's it, I'm calling the Sheriff!

>   (HE turns to exit. KK stops HIM, pleads.)

KK

Please, don't call, I promise I'll get him to stop. He's a man of great
passion; he doesn't mean to disturb anyone. But what I'm about to
do is disturbing him, can't you see? Anybody in this motel, even
the one's who can't sleep on account of us are bound to understand
if they just knew the cross he's bearing! Please, sir, I promise I can
get him to quiet his prayers.

MM

I want *silent* prayers, and I'm going back to my office, and then I'll
give you one minute to shut him up.

BW

O Lord, hear my prayer on this evening of testing and tribulation!

KK

>   (Grabbing MM's arm before HE exits.)

Please, I beg you, sir, don't call the Sheriff. I promise to quiet
him down.

MM

Shut him up.

>   (MM exits. KK crosses to BW. HE is still on HIS knees.)

BW

And Lord, let this servant refrain from the hasty intervention of the
Sheriff, and let my heart be quieted with Thy presence!

>   (KK sighs. Stands beside BW.)

KK

I want you to get up off your knees and promise me you'll quiet down. Please, Mister Walters. I promise I won't leave tonight if you just stop shouting at God and anyone else who'll hear and talk softly to me. It's too late for any shouting.

  (BW gets up, brushes the dust off the knees of HIS trousers.)

BW

Well, amen then.

  (KK finds a chair and pulls it to one side of the room.
  SHE looks at BW, HE at HER. KK sits down and turns
  HER head away.)

KK

You ever plead on your knees, shouting to God, with Jessie?

BW

I asked you not to mention her name again. So, you're stayin' tonight?

KK

Yes, I don't want you arrested for praying too loud.

BW

Thank you, Miss Kathryn.

KK

But I'll be staying right here in this chair until I'm tired enough to sleep on the floor.

BW

So, you're not gonna take nothing off? I mean, ya' got a nightgown that's right here, and I promise I won't look.

KK

No, Mister Walters, I'm going to sleep in my wedding dress.

  (BW crosses to HER.)

BW

(Getting loud again.)

No, no, I insist that you take the bed and I'll take the chair and then the floor.

KK

Mister Walters, I'm afraid we need to be quieter.

BW

(Quieter.)

I insist that if you're gonna spend one night and prolong our marriage another few hours that you take the marriage bed. I remain a chivalrous man and a man very much in love with his bride.

(Volume rising.)

Love suffers long and is kind, beareth all things, believeth all things, hopeth all things, endureth all things.

KK

Yes, the love chapter in First Corinthians is a lovely confession. But we still need to quiet down. I'm sorry.

BW

(Quieter.)

But please, it's only right that I take the chair and the floor tonight. I promise I won't look, and I won't touch ya', I promise. I'll take all my things away from the bed . . .

(BW gets HIS luggage and whatever else is strewn near the bed and brings them to the chair.)

BW (cont'd)

And bring them over to the chair and I'll be fine just knowin' I'm in the same room with my Kate, though maybe for just one final night.

KK

It's alright, but—

BW

      (Falling to HIS knees.)

O but I insist and plead with you for the sake of my dignity. No woman should sleep on a hard floor while a man has the comfort of a bed. No, it ain't chivalrous, it ain't dignified, it ain't Christian.

      (KK concedes and crosses to the foot of the bed and sits. BW sits in the chair.)

BW (cont'd)

Now that's better.

      (Extended PAUSE. They don't look at each other.)

BW (cont'd)

I don't really mean "better," probably just more appropriate.

      (PAUSE.)

BW (cont'd)

Come to think of it, "appropriate" ain't the word, either.

KK

Well, as long as it's a quiet word, Mister Walters.

BW

Yes, ma'am.

      (Extended PAUSE.)

BW (cont'd)

Sure is a pretty night.

KK

Yes, it even warmed up a little.

BW

So ya' didn't need your coat, did ya'?

KK

No, it was lovely.

BW

It's funny that you'd be leavin' me in the night, and despite all the turmoil in your soul, you noticed the weather, that it was warmer.

KK

Being forced without a coat makes you notice the weather.

BW

I'm sorry 'bout that, Miss Kate. I thought it the right thing at the time.

KK

I wouldn't have noticed the warmth otherwise.

BW

I guess there ain't no interruptin' the sovereignty of God.

KK

That's true.

      (PAUSE.)

BW

See, we can have a theological discussion that's quiet enough for tonight.

KK

Yes.

BW

You don't suppose he called the Sheriff, did he?

KK

Hope not.

BW

Can't imagine spendin' my weddin' night in jail on account of loud prayin'.

KK

No.

> (Extended PAUSE. KK lifts HER veil but does not face BW.)

KK (cont'd)

Mister Walters.

BW

Yes.

KK

I hope it's alright if I ask you a few more questions.

BW

Fire away. I'm just glad I get to hear your voice tonight.

> (PAUSE.)

KK

Your two boys, Herbert and Sammy?

BW

What about 'em? I love those boys.

KK

The little one's Sammy, right?

BW

Six years old on his last birthday. Why?

KK

Did he ever have a blue, little two-wheeler bike?

BW

He got it on his last birthday; one of the wealthier families in our home church got it for 'im. Ol' boy was so excited it was like he'd never got nothin' else in his life. Why?

KK

He ever break any bones?

BW

Yeh. Doesn't every little boy at one time or other? Truth is I was holdin' 'im walkin' down our front steps, just 'bout two or three steps on that porch, and, sure enough, I tripped and little Sammy went flyin'. I ripped my trousers and he landed on his arm and broke it. That little boy didn't cry hardly a whimper. But he sure enough broke his arm. I blamed myself for that. Who knows why a man trips over stairs he's climbed a thousand times? So why you wanna know all about Sammy all of a sudden?

(PAUSE.)

KK

I had a dream, Mister Walters. Last night I had a dream.

BW

About Sammy?

KK

He was on a blue bicycle. He had a cast on his arm and was crying.

BW

Really?

KK

Said his momma told him his daddy's left and wasn't coming back.

BW

Dreams can be strange sometimes, can't they?

KK

And I dreamed the same thing three times. Woke up after each time, fell back asleep and dreamed the same dream. Sammy on his blue bike, with a broken arm, crying for you.

BW

So, what d'ya think it means? You probably feelin' a little sorry 'cause ya' think you're takin' me from my boys. But you didn't take 'em from me, she did.

KK

It's the weight, Mister Walters. He kept asking me where you were. I kept lying and telling little Sammy I didn't know. But I did know and wouldn't tell him. I was going to Iowa with his daddy, and he was staying in Texas. I've never been a liar before, Mister Walters; but I lied like the devil in that dream.

BW

So, what are ya' sayin'? Your dreams mean more than my word and the truth?

KK

I've had visions before. Visions of the church and where it would be built and what it should look like. Visions of a ministry in Colorado. I've even had a vision of me in a wedding dress playing on a bed like a little girl, falling back on the mattress like I was slain. All of them have materialized, except the last one. But I've never before had such a dream. And it scares me, Mister Walters.

BW

And I've dreamt I was President Roosevelt. That don't make it so.

KK

You mean God never used dreams?

BW

Of course, he did: Joseph in the Bible—both Josephs, in fact. Can't think of anytime else off hand. And Sammy, though I love 'im, sure ain't no Joseph. And Iowa ain't Jerusalem, and Denver ain't Egypt.

(PAUSE.)

KK

(Not interrogative, quietly.)

Why would a woman with no job and two little boys abandon a God-fearing, servant of the Lord? Why?

BW

We've already gone over that. I've in faith put my hand to this marital plow and I ain't lookin' back.

(Longer PAUSE.)

KK

A little boy on a blue bike and a cast on his arm, crying, asking for his dad. And I say I don't know where he is.

BW

And I was Franklin D. Roosevelt givin' an inaugural address.

(PAUSE.)

KK

I guess I really *don't* know where you are, Mister Walters.

BW

In Iowa, across the room on our wedding night.

(PAUSE.)

KK

Wedding night.

BW

Yep.

KK

I'm ready to go to sleep, Mister Walters. I've decided to keep my dress on.

BW

That's plenty fine, Miss Kathryn; I'll be here in the chair.

(KK lies down. Long PAUSE.)

KK

Good-night, Mister Walters.

BW

Good-night, Miss Kathryn.

    (PAUSE.)

KK

Mister Walters, would ya' mind if I turned off the lamp?

    (BW jumps up, goes to turn off the lamp.)

BW

I'll get it for ya'.

    (BW turns off light. Both characters are seen dimly.)

KK

Thank you. I think I want to sleep now.

BW

You go to sleep.

    (PAUSE.)

KK

I'm still planning on returning to Denver tomorrow.

    (PAUSE.)

BW

Therefore, do not worry about tomorrow, for tomorrow will worry about its own things. Sufficient for the day is its own trouble.

    (PAUSE.)

KK

And I'm afraid Little Sammy's going to come again tonight.

    (PAUSE.)

BW

Don't pay it no mind, Miss Kathryn, don't pay it no mind.

    (LIGHTS completely out, a long PAUSE.)

    (SIX SLIDES ARE SHOWN ON THE BACK WALL:)

    (SLIDE ONE: Kathryn did leave Burroughs that night and returned to Denver.

    (SLIDE TWO: Her Denver congregation, feeling betrayed by her departure, had already moved on and found another pastor. This forced Kathryn back into Burroughs' arms.)

    (SLIDE THREE: The marriage lasted seven years.)

    (SLIDE FOUR: A Kathryn Kuhlman biographer found Burroughs' first wife, Jessie. She disputed Burroughs' story and claims that he left her and their two boys. Throughout the remainder of his life, Burroughs never visited his two sons.)

    (SLIDE FIVE: Kathryn Kuhlman would become a most influential faith healer and evangelist, filling arenas throughout the country in the 1950s, 60s, and 70s.)

    (SLIDE SIX: Kathryn Kuhlman died in 1976.)

THE END

9 781959 685272